Easy How-to Techniques for
SIMPLY STYLISH
18" DOLLS™

Designs by Andra Knight-Bowman

Annie's®

Introduction

This exciting new book is a practical guide designed to teach you indispensable knitting techniques that apply to 18-inch doll clothes. You'll find a collection of outfits that are easy and quick to make, along with seven complete technique lessons and seven stylish 18-inch doll ensembles. With each method you learn, you'll be able to immediately apply it. These are examples of what you'll learn: how to work cables so you can create fabrics that look complicated but are very easy to work, how to knit in the round and how to work a jogless join for stripes. Knitters who find seaming daunting will learn the 3-Needle Bind-Off, a foolproof no-sew method for joining edges. Finally, we will teach you how to embellish any knitted fabric with delightful embroidered accents that will add a bit of color and personality to your projects.

Many of the deisgns in this book are made using either a circular needle or double-point needles. There are also patterns that are worked back and forth. Circular needles are suggested for ease and comfort. Each lesson starts with easy to understand step-by-step illustrations and instructions. Then, you can test your skills by making an outfit for your 18-inch doll with the pattern that follows.

You'll find that learning knitting techniques and applying them on small projects such as 18-inch doll clothes allows you to grasp new techniques fast and, as a result, you'll be left with little outfits that can be created effortlessly in just one weekend!

Meet the Designer

At the age of 7, I learned to knit, and was a natural at the craft. I soon started making sweaters for my Barbie dolls and my dog, Mitzi. Designing entered my life at an early age.

In high school, I had the opportunity to work at a local yarn shop. It was there I learned about fibers and sweater designing. My goal in life was to own a yarn shop of my own.

I opened Knits & Pearls in 2004 and introduced many of my designs from previous years to my customers. Since then I have created many more designs. They have been published in numerous magazines and books, including *Easy Cable Knits for All Seasons*, *Modular Knitting Made Easy*, *Fun to Knit Doll Clothes* and *Seamless (or Nearly Seamless) Knits*. I feel so blessed and am grateful for everyone who has believed in me.

I reside in Johnson City, Tenn., with my wonderful husband, Terry, who has been a gem through book writings, and two furry kids (cats), Billie and Blue. I just couldn't ask for a better life!

—Andra Knight-Bowman

Table of Contents

Lesson 1: Knitting in the Round With Double-Point Needles

Double-point needles come in handy for working small circumference projects such as the cuff on a sock, mittens or the shaping on the top of a hat, and of course—adorable 18-inch doll clothes! Double-point needles are commonly used in sets of four or five. If you're new to working with these kinds of needles, take a deep breath, relax and give yourself some time to get the hang of using them, because they have so many valuable uses.

When working in the round on double-point needles, you will divide your work evenly among three or four needles, and the fourth (or fifth) needle will be your "working needle." Most double-point needles are about 6–9 inches long, but very short (4-inch) needles are available from specialty sources. These are especially useful when working mitten thumbs or fingers on gloves.

You may feel awkward the first time you use double-point needles but that awkwardness will disappear quickly as you become more comfortable manipulating multiple needles.

Working with Four Double-Point needles

Cast on the number of stitches required. Distribute the stitches as instructed in the pattern on 3 double-point needles. Position the needles so that needle 1 is on the left and needle 3 is on the right.

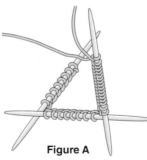

Figure A

The yarn you're about to work with should be attached to the last stitch on needle 3.

Join the stitches into a circle by inserting a free needle into the first cast-on stitch on needle 1 and knitting it. Continue knitting across needle 1 until all stitches have been knit. The stitches that were

originally on needle 1 will now be on what had been the "free" needle and needle 1 will become your working needle. Turn the triangle and use the free needle to knit across the stitches on needle 2. Continue in this manner, working around the three needles that are holding the stitches. Note that you will be only using two needles at a time—you can just ignore the other two needles.

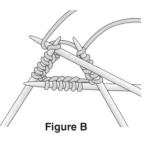

Figure B

Working With Five Double-Point needles

Cast on the number of stitches required. Distribute stitches evenly on 4 double-point needles. Position the needles so that needle 1 is on the left and needle 4 is on the right. The yarn you're about to work with should be attached to the last stitch on needle 4.

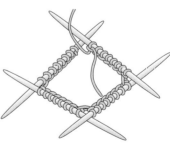

Figure C

Join the stitches into a circle by using a free needle to knit the first cast-on stitch on needle 1. Continue working around the needles as you did when working with four needles.

Double-Point Dottie

Finished Measurements
Chest: 10¾ inches
Sweater length: 6 inches
Shorts length: 5 inches

Materials
- Cascade Yarns Cascade 220 (worsted weight; 100% Peruvian highland wool; 220 yds/100g per ball): 1 ball each white #8505 (A), dark lavender #8887 (B), Christmas red #8895 (C) and goldenrod #7827 (D)
- Size 5 (3.75mm) straight and double-point needles (set of 4)
- Size 7 (4.5mm) double-point needles (set of 4) or size needed to obtain gauge
- Stitch marker

Gauge
20 sts and 25 rows/rnds = 4 inches/10cm in St st with larger needles.

To save time, take time to check gauge.

Special Abbreviations
Make 1 Left (M1L): Insert LH needle from front to back under the running thread between the last st worked and next st on LH needle; knit into the back of resulting loop.

Make 1 Right (M1R): Insert LH needle from back to front under the running thread between the last st worked and next st on LH needle. With RH needle, knit into the front of resulting loop.

Pattern Note
Shorts are worked from the waist down.

Sweater

Body
With smaller dpns and A, cast on 54 sts; mark beg of rnd and join, taking care not to twist sts.

[Purl 1 rnd, knit 1 rnd] twice.

Change to larger dpns; work even in St st until piece measures 3½ inches.

Back
Row 1 (RS): K27, turn, leaving rem 27 sts unworked on single dpn or waste yarn.

Work 3 rows even.

Shape Sleeves
Inc row (RS): K1, M1R, knit to last st, M1L, k1—29 sts.

Rep Inc row [every RS row] 5 times, ending with a WS row—39 sts.

Transfer first and last 13 sts to waste yarn for shoulders and center 13 sts to waste yarn for back neck.

Front
With RS facing, rejoin A to work rem 27 sts.

Work 2 rows in St st.

Shape Sleeves & V-Neck
Row 1 (RS): K13; put center st on hold; join 2nd ball of yarn and k13—13 sts each side.

Row 2: Working both sides at once with separate balls of yarn, purl across.

Row 3: K1, M1R, k9, k2tog, k1; k1, ssk, k9, M1L, k1.

Rep [Rows 2 and 3] 5 times.

Place 13 sts on holder for each side.

Finishing
Join shoulders using 3-needle bind-off (see Lesson 3 on page 12).

Neck Band
With B and smaller dpns, starting at left shoulder seam, pick up and knit 11 sts along front neck to center of V-neck, k1 from holder, pick up and knit 11 sts along front neck edge to shoulder, k13 back neck sts; distribute sts on 3 dpns, mark beg of rnd and join.

Purl 1 rnd, knit 1 rnd, purl 1 rnd.

Bind off loosely.

Sleeve Bands
With B and smaller dpns, starting at center underarm, pick up and knit 27 sts around armhole; distribute sts evenly on 3 dpns, mark beg of rnd and join.

Purl 1 rnd, knit 1 rnd, purl 1 rnd.

Bind off loosely.

Weave in ends.

Shorts
With B and smaller dpns, cast on 52 sts; mark beg of rnd and join, taking care not to twist sts. [Purl 1 rnd, knit 1 rnd] twice.

Change to larger dpns; work in St st until piece measures 2 inches.

Inc rnd: K25, M1L, k1, M1R, k26—54 sts.

Knit 3 rnds.

Inc rnd: K26, M1L, k1, M1R, k27—56 sts.

Knit 3 rnds.

Inc rnd: K27, M1L, k1, M1R, k28—58 sts.

Knit 3 rnds.

Work even until piece measures 4 inches.

Left Leg
Rnd 1: K29; transfer rem 29 sts to waste yarn.

Distribute left leg sts evenly on 3 dpns, mark beg of rnd and join.

Dec rnd: Knit to last 2 sts, k2tog—28 sts.

Knit 1 rnd, then rep Dec rnd—27 sts.

Change to smaller dpns; purl 1 rnd, knit 1 rnd, purl 1 rnd.

Bind off loosely.

Right Leg
Transfer 29 right leg sts evenly distributed to 3 dpns, mark beg of rnd and join.

Rnd 1: Knit.

Dec rnd: Ssk, knit to end—28 sts.

Knit 1 rnd, rep Dec rnd—27 sts.

Change to smaller dpns; purl 1 rnd, knit 1 rnd, purl 1 rnd.

Bind off loosely.

Weave in ends.

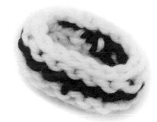

Wrist Bands
Make 2

With smaller straight needles, long-tail cast-on and A, cast on 15 sts.

Knit 1 row with A, knit 2 rows with C, knit 2 rows with A.

Bind off loosely.

Sew side seam.

Weave in ends.

Knee Brace
With smaller needle and D, cast on 18 sts.

Work in St st for 2 inches.

Bind off loosely.

Sew side seam.

Weave in ends. •

Head Band
With smaller straight needles, long-tail cast-on and A, cast on 45 sts.

Knit 1 row with A, knit 2 rows with C, knit 2 rows with A.

Bind off loosely.

Sew side seam.

Weave in ends.

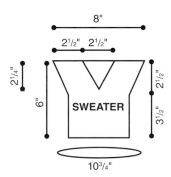

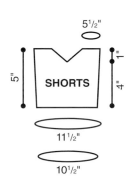

Lesson 2: So Simple Circular Knitting

Don't be hesitant to give circular knitting a try. The project that follows will give you a taste of how enjoyable seamless knitting is. We promise that once you get started, you'll enjoy the rhythmic motion that knitting in the round provides. Just cast on and round and round you go—you may not want to stop!

Casting Onto a Circular Needle

Step 1: After casting on the required number of stitches, place your work down on a flat surface, making sure the cast-on edge faces the center. This will ensure that your stitches do not twist around the needle.

Step 2: Place a marker on the right-hand needle so that you'll remember the location of the beginning of the round. Then join the stitches into a circle by knitting into the first stitch that you cast on.

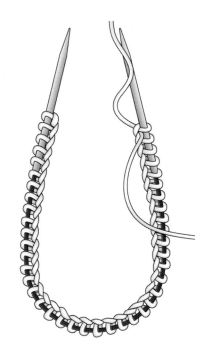

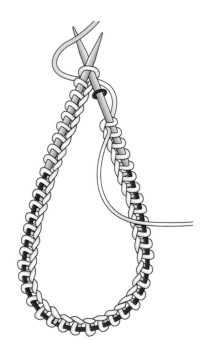

T!P

Try this handy trick:
When working your first round, to keep your stitches from twisting around the needle, try using several clothespins to hold the stitches in place, removing them as you work.

Circular Suzie

Skill Level

◼◼◼▢ INTERMEDIATE

Finished Measurements

Capelet width (at bottom): 15¾ inches
Caplete length: 4 inches
Skirt length: 5 inches

Materials

- Patons Kroy Socks (fingering weight; 75% washable wool/25% nylon; 166 yds/50g per ball): 1 ball each sweet stripes #55315 (MC) and gentry gray #55042 (CC)
- Size 3 (3.25mm) 16-inch circular needle and double-point needles
- Size 4 (3.5mm) 16-inch circular and double-point needles (set of 5) or size needed to obtain gauge
- 7 stitch markers, 1 in CC for beg of rnd
- Cable needle
- 5 (½-inch) buttons
- 1 foot ⅛-inch-wide elastic

Gauge

24 sts and 32 rows/rnds = 4 inches/10cm in St st with larger needles.

To save time, take time to check gauge.

Special Technique

I-Cord: *K4, do not turn, slip sts back to LH needle; rep from * until cord is desired length. Bind off.

Capelet

Body

With smaller needle and MC, cast on 94 sts; do not join.

Knit 3 rows.

Next row (RS): Change to larger needle; k15, pm, k22, pm, k26, pm, k22, pm, k9.

Work in St st for 2 inches, ending with a WS row.

Dec row (RS): [Knit to 2 sts before marker, k2tog, sm, ssk] 4 times, knit to end—86 sts.

Work 3 rows even.

Rep [last 4 rows] twice, then rep Dec row [every RS row] 3 times, ending with a WS row—46 sts.

Change to smaller needle and knit 4 rows.

Bind off loosely; do not cut yarn.

Finishing
Weave in ends. Block.

Buttonband
With RS facing and using smaller needle, pick up and knit 30 sts along left front edge.

Knit 3 rows.

Bind off loosely.

Buttonhole Band
With RS facing, using smaller needle and beg at bottom, pick up and knit 30 sts along right front edge.

Knit 1 row.

Buttonhole row (RS): K3, [yo, k2og, k6] 3 times, yo, k2tog, k1.

Knit 1 row.

Bind off loosely.

Sew buttons opposite buttonholes.

Skirt
With smaller circular needle and CC, cast on 120 sts; pm for beg of rnd and join, taking care not to twist sts.

Purl 1 rnd, knit 1 rnd, purl 1 rnd.

Next rnd: Change to larger needle; k23, pm, [k12, pm] twice, k25, [pm, k12] twice, pm, k24.

Next rnd: Slipping markers when you come to them, [knit to marker, sl 1] 6 times, knit to end of rnd.

Next rnd: Knit around.

Rep last 2 rnds until piece measures 4 inches.

Pleating rnd: Knit to 6 sts before marker, *slip 6 sts to cn and hold in back, remove marker; [knit 1 st from LH needle and 1 st from cn tog] 6 times; rep from * twice; knit to next marker, **remove marker, slip 6 sts to cn and hold in front, [knit 1 st from cn and 1 st from LH needle tog] 6 times; rep from ** twice, knit to end—84 sts.

Note: Change to dpns if sts no longer fit comfortably on circular needle.

Knit 1 rnd.

Change to smaller dpns and knit 5 rnds.

Turning ridge: Purl around.

Knit 5 rnds.

Bind off loosely.

Finishing

Overlap ends of elastic and sew tog to make an 11-inch circle.

Fold waistband down along turning ridge, covering elastic.

Sew bound-off edge to WS.

Messenger Bag

With larger dpns and CC, cast on 6 sts.

Knit 24 rows.

Rnd 1: K6; with 2nd needle, pick up and knit 12 sts along side of piece; with 3rd needle, pick up and knit 6 sts along cast-on edge; with 4th needle, pick up and knit 12 sts along side of piece—36 sts.

Rnd 2: Purl.

Rnd 3: [Sl 1, k4, sl 1, k12] twice.

Rnd 4: Knit.

Rep Rnds 3 and 4 until piece measures 1½ inches from Rnd 1.

Purl 1 rnd.

Bind off 24, knit to end—12 sts.

Knit 20 rows.

Buttonhole row: K6, yo, k2tog, k4.

Knit 5 rows.

Bind off loosely.

Finishing

Strap
Pick up and knit 4 sts along top short side.

Work 13-inch I-Cord.

Bind off loosely.

Sew I-cord to opposite short side.

Sew button to center front of bag. ●

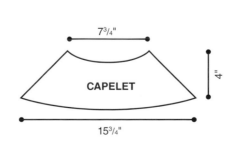

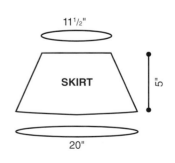

Lesson 3: The Practical & Simple 3-Needle Bind-Off

You'll find that this bind-off has several practical uses. In certain patterns, this method is used to join the front and back shoulders of a sweater. What makes this bind-off special is that it's also classified as a finishing technique because it creates a neat and solid seam.

Step 1: Hold the live stitches on two separate needles with right sides of the fabric together.

Step 2: Use a third needle to knit the first stitch on the front needle together with the first stitch on the back needle.

Repeat, knitting the next front and back stitches together. There are now two stitches on the right-hand needle; pass the first stitch over the second to bind it off.

Continue in this manner, knitting together a stitch from each needle, then binding off one stitch, until one stitch remains on the right-hand needle. Fasten off the last stitch by pulling the yarn through it.

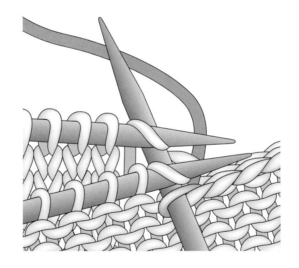

> **T!P**
> It's important that you start off with the same number of stitches on both of the pieces that you're working in order for the stitches to line up accurately. Since this technique is commonly used when joining two separate pieces together, it's necessary that the stitch counts match.

3-Needle Nettie

Skill Level

◼◼◼◻ INTERMEDIATE

Finished Measurements
Chest: 11½ inches
Length: 9 inches

Materials
- Plymouth Yarn Encore Worsted (worsted weight; 75% acrylic/ 25% wool; 200 yds/100g per ball): 1 ball hot pink #137 (MC)
- Plymouth Yarn Baby Alpaca Ultimo (super chunky weight; 90% baby alpaca/10% nylon; 109 yds/100g per ball): 1 ball natural #100 (CC)
- Size 7 (4.5mm) straight and double-point needles (set of 4) or size needed to obtain gauge
- 7 stitch markers, 1 in CC for beg of rnd
- 3 hook-and-eye closures

Gauge
20 sts and 25 rows = 4 inches in St st with MC.

To save time, take time to check gauge.

Special Technique
I-Cord: *K3, do not turn, slip sts back to LH needle; rep from * until cord is desired length. Bind off.

Pattern Note
Body of coat is worked in one piece to the underarm, then back and fronts are worked separately. After the shoulders are joined, the sleeve is picked up around the armhole and worked in the round to the cuff.

Coat

Body
With straight needles and CC, cast on 29 sts.

Knit 4 rows.

Inc row (RS): Change to MC; kfb in each st across—58 sts.

Work in St st until piece measures 5 inches, ending with a WS row.

Dec row (RS): Change to CC; k2tog across—29 sts.

Knit 1 row.

Inc row (RS): Change to MC; kfb in each st across—58 sts.

Purl 1 row.

Right Front
Row 1 (RS): K14, turn, leaving rem sts unworked on needle.

Work in St st until armhole measures 3 inches, ending with a RS row.

Next row (WS): P9, bind off 5 sts for front neck.

Transfer rem 9 sts to waste yarn for shoulder.

Back
Row 1 (RS): Rejoin MC with RS facing; k30, turn, leaving rem sts unworked.

Work in St st until armhole measures 3 inches.

Transfer first and last 9 sts to pieces of waste yarn for shoulders and center 12 sts to waste yarn for back neck. Cut yarn, leaving a 12-inch tail.

Left Front
Row 1 (RS): Rejoin MC with RS facing; knit to end.

Work in St st until armhole measures 3 inches, ending with a RS row.

Bind off 5 sts for front neck, p9.

Cut yarn, leaving a 12-inch tail.

Join front and back shoulders using 3-needle bind-off (see Lesson 3 on page 12).

Sleeves
With dpns and MC and beg at bottom of armhole, pick up and knit 30 sts around armhole, distributing sts evenly on 3 dpns; mark beg of rnd and join.

Knit all rnds until sleeve measures 3 inches.

Easy How-to Techniques for Simply Stylish 18" Dolls

Hat

Body

With CC and dpns, cast on 28 sts; distribute evenly on 3 dpns, mark beg of rnd and join, taking care not to twist sts.

[Knit 1 rnd, purl 1 rnd] twice.

Inc rnd: Change to MC; kfb in each st across—56 sts.

Knit 5 rnds and on last rnd, [k8, pm] 7 times (7th marker is beg of rnd marker).

Dec rnd: [Knit to 2 sts before marker, k2tog] 7 times—49 sts.

Rep Dec rnd [every other rnd] 6 times, ending with a Dec rnd—7 sts.

Change to CC; k2tog around—15 sts.

Purl 1 rnd, knit 1 rnd, purl 1 rnd.

Bind off loosely.

Finishing

Right Band
With CC, pick up and knit 28 sts along right front edge.

Knit 4 rows.

Bind off loosely.

Left Band
Work as for right band.

Collar
With WS facing and using CC, starting at the base of left front band, pick up and knit 6 sts along front neck, k12 back neck sts, pick up and knit 6 sts along front neck—24 sts.

Knit 4 rows.

Bind off loosely.

Mark positions for 3 hook-and-eye closures at inside of each front band, with first being 1½ inches from top of band and 2nd being 1½ inches from bottom edge, and 3rd being between the first 2.

Sew hook-and-eye closures at the markers.

Cut yarn, leaving a 6-inch tail.

With tapestry needle, thread tail through rem sts and pull tight.

Weave in tails.

Ear Flaps

With CC and dpn, pick up and knit 5 sts along cast-on edge.

Knit 8 rows.

Dec row: K2tog, k1, k2tog—3 sts.

Change to MC; work a 3-st I-cord for 9 inches.

Bind off loosely.

Work 2nd ear flap on opposite side of hat.

Make 3 (2-inch) pompoms (page 46).

Sew one to end of each I-cord and at top of crown.

Boots

With MC and dpns, cast on 7 sts.

Knit 22 rows.

Rnd 1: K7, pick up and knit 11 sts along side edge, 4 sts along cast-on edge, and 11 sts along side edge; distribute sts among 3 dpns, mark beg of rnd and join—33 sts.

Knit 4 rnds.

Dec rnd: K1, k2tog, k1, ssk, knit to end of rnd—31 sts.

Knit 1 rnd.

Dec rnd: K2tog, k1, ssk, knit to end of rnd—29 sts.

Next rnd: Change to CC; k3, [k2tog] 13 times—16 sts.

Work in garter st (purl 1 rnd, knit 1 rnd) for 2½ inches.

Bind off loosely.

Weave in ends. ●

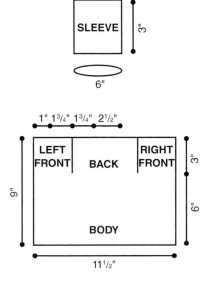

Lesson 4: Magical Jogless Stripes

This indispensable technique will help you avoid the "color jog" that occurs at the beginning of a round when working stripes. You will find this little trick useful when making striped hats, mittens or sweaters.

When we knit in the round, we are actually creating a very long spiral of stitches, so the first stitch of the round is always lower in the spiral than the last stitch of the round. This is very apparent when we make stripes in the round because the color changes accentuate the offset of these two stitches and there's a very visible jog. There are a few different methods of disguising this jog, but this one is the easiest.

When you change colors, knit the entire first round with the new color, stopping at the beginning-of-round marker. Now, slip the first stitch of the second round of the new color purlwise, and then continue knitting around. It's that simple! By slipping that first stitch of the second round, you are hiking the stitch up a little bit and making it even with the last stitch of the first round.

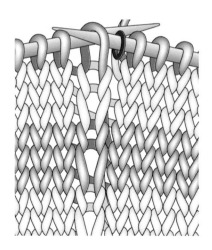

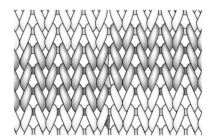

The drawing above shows how your knitting would look if you did not work the jogless join technique. As you can see, it leaves uneven group of stitches on each round where a color change occurs.

Jogless Jenny

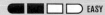

Finished Measurements
Sweater circumference: 13¼ inches
Sweater length: 8½ inches
Leggings length: 7½ inches

Materials
- Universal Yarn Uptown Worsted (worsted weight; 100% acrylic; 203 yds/113g per ball): 1 ball each chocolate brown #321 (MC) and lime #314 (CC)
- Size 5 (3.75mm) 16-inch circular and double-point needles (set of 4)
- Size 7 (4.5mm) 16-inch circular and double-point needles (set of 4) or size needed to obtain gauge
- Stitch markers
- Stitch holders
- 2 snap closures

4 MEDIUM

Gauge
18 sts and 25 rnds/rows = 4 inches/10cm in St st with larger needle.

To save time, take time to check gauge.

Special Abbreviations
Make 1 Left (M1L): Insert LH needle from front to back under the running thread between the last st worked and next st on LH needle; knit into the back of resulting loop.

Make 1 Right (M1R): Insert LH needle from back to front under the running thread between the last st worked and next st on LH needle. With RH needle, knit into the front of resulting loop.

Slip, slip, purl (ssp): Slip next 2 sts 1 at a time kwise, slip sts back to LH needle and p2tog-tbl.

Pattern Notes

Body of sweater is worked in the round to under-arms, then front and back are worked separately back and forth. After shoulders are joined, sleeves are picked up from armhole and worked in the round to the cuff.

Leggings are worked from the waist down.

Sweater

Body

With smaller dpns and MC, cast on 60 sts; distribute sts evenly among 3 dpns, mark beg of rnd and join, taking care not to twist sts.

Purl 1 rnd, knit 1 rnd, purl 1 rnd.

Change to larger dpns and CC; work in St st, alternating CC and MC every 2 rnds (slipping first st of 2nd rnd of each stripe) until piece measures 5½ inches.

Back

K30, turn, leaving rem sts on a single dpn or waste yarn for front.

Maintaining stripe pat, work back and forth until armhole measures 3 inches, ending with a RS row.

Next row (WS): Bind off 10 sts for left shoulder, purl to end—20 sts.

Transfer first 10 sts to waste yarn for right shoulder and 2nd 10 sts to separate waste yarn for back neck.

Front

With RS facing, rejoin yarn.

Maintaining stripe pat, work back and forth until armhole measures 2 inches, ending with a WS row.

Shape Neck

Row 1 (RS): K12, transfer center 6 sts to waste yarn for front neck, join 2nd ball of yarn and knit to end.

Row 2: Purl to 2 sts before neck edge, ssp; p2tog, purl to end—11 sts each side.

Row 3: Knit to 2 sts before neck edge, k2tog; ssk, knit to end—10 sts each side.

Work even until armhole measures 3 inches.

Transfer left shoulder sts to waste yarn.

Finishing

Weave in ends.

Join right shoulder using 3-needle bind-off (see Lesson 3 on page 12).

Collar

With WS facing, using smaller circular needle and MC, k10 back neck sts, pick up and knit 7 sts along right front neck edge, k6 front neck sts, pick up and knit 7 sts along left neck edge—30 sts.

Knit 3 rows.

Inc row: [K2, M1] 14 times, k2—44 sts.

Knit 3 rows.

Change to larger needle and knit 6 rows.

Bind off loosely.

Left Shoulder Closure

With RS facing, using smaller needle and MC, knit across left shoulder sts.

Knit 2 rows.

Bind off loosely.

Sew 2 snaps evenly spaced on front and back left shoulders.

Sleeves

With larger dpns and MC, beg at bottom of armhole, pick up and knit 26 sts evenly around armhole; mark beg of rnd and join.

Work in stripe pat, alternating MC and CC every 2 rnds (slipping first st of 2nd rnd of each stripe) until sleeve measures 2½ inches.

Dec rnd: Change to smaller dpns; with MC, [k2, k2tog] 6 times, k2—20 sts.

Purl 1 rnd, knit 1 rnd, purl 1 rnd.

Bind off loosely.

Rep for other sleeve.

Weave in ends.

Leggings

With smaller dpns and MC, cast on 50 sts; mark beg of rnd and join, taking care not to twist sts.

Purl 1 rnd, knit 1 rnd, purl 1 rnd.

Change to larger dpns; work in St st for 2 inches.

Inc rnd: K24, M1L, k1, M1R, k25—52 sts.

Knit 3 rnds.

Inc rnd: K25, M1L, k1, M1R, k26—54 sts.

Knit 3 rnds.

Inc rnd: K26, M1L, k1, M1R, k27—56 sts.

Knit 3 rnds.

Work even until piece measures 4 inches.

Left Leg

Change to larger dpns; k28, leaving rem 28 sts unworked on dpn or waste yarn.

Distribute left leg sts evenly on 3 dpns, mark beg of rnd and join.

Knit 1 rnd.

Dec rnd: Knit to last 2 sts, k2tog—27 sts.

Rep Dec rnd [every other rnd] 5 times—22 sts.

Work even until leg measures 3¼ inches.

Change to smaller dpns; purl 1 rnd, knit 1 rnd, purl 1 rnd.

Bind off loosely.

Right Leg

With RS facing, rejoin yarn; with larger dpns, k28, distributing sts evenly on 3 dpns; mark beg of rnd and join.

Knit 1 rnd.

Dec rnd: Ssk, knit to end—27 sts.

Rep Dec rnd [every other rnd] 5 times—22 sts.

Work even until leg measures 3¼ inches.

Change to smaller dpns; purl 1 rnd, knit 1 rnd, purl 1 rnd.

Bind off loosely.

Weave in ends. Block.

Skull Cap

With smaller dpns and MC, cast on 60 sts; distribute evenly on 3 dpns, mark beg of rnd and join, taking care not to twist sts.

Work in 2x2 rib for 3 inches.

Dec rnd: [K2tog, p2tog] 30 times—30 sts.

Next rnd: [K1, p1] 30 times.

Next rnd: K2tog 15 times—15 sts.

Cut yarn, leaving a 6-inch tail. Using tapestry needle, thread tail through rem sts, and pull tight.

Weave in all ends. ●

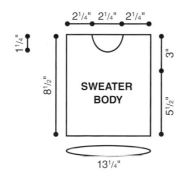

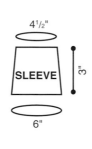

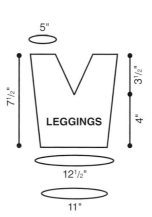

Lesson 5: Cables in 3 Easy Steps

Cables are much easier to create than they appear. All you need is some yarn, a cable needle and the knitting needles of your choice. Then, test your cablemaking skills with confidence when you make the Cabled KatieBeth sweater on the following page.

There are just three easy steps for working a basic cable.

Step 1: Slide stitches onto a cable needle to hold them out of the way temporarily.

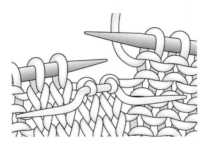

Step 2: Work the next stitches on the left-hand needle.

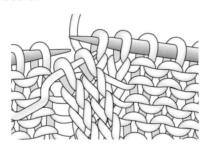

Step 3: Work the stitches from the cable needle.

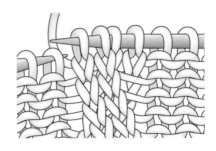

The pattern will always be specific as to how many stitches to slide onto the cable needle. It also will tell you whether the cable needle is to be held in front or in back of the work. This is very important because this is what causes the cable to twist to the left or to the right.

> **T!P**
>
> **Making Sense of Cable Charts**
> Once you learn how to read a cable chart, it will be much easier to "visually" understand how to work a cable pattern. The chart on page 29 illustrates what the cable pattern looks like for the Cabled KatieBeth sweater and the key explains what each symbol on the chart means.

Cabled KatieBeth

Finished Measurements
Chest: 11 inches
Sweater length: 6½ inches
Skirt length: 7 inches

Materials
- Berroco Vintage DK (DK; 50% acrylic/ 40% wool/10% nylon; 288 yds/ 100g per ball): 1 ball each mochi #2101 (MC) and cracked pepper #2107 (CC)
- Size 4 (3.5mm) needles
- Size 6 (4mm) needles or size needed to obtain gauge
- Stitch markers
- Cable needle
- 5 (½-inch) buttons
- 2 snap closures

Gauge
22 sts and 28 rows = 4 inches/10cm in St st with larger needles.

To save time, take time to check gauge.

Special Abbreviations
1 over 1 Right Cross (1/1 RC): Sl 1 to cn and hold in back, k1, k1 from cn.

1 over 1 Left Cross (1/1 LC): Sl 1 to cn and hold in front, k1, k1 from cn.

2 over 1 Right Cross (2/1 RC): Sl 1 to cn and hold in back, k2, k1 from cn.

2 over 1 Right Purl Cross (2/1 RPC): Sl 1 to cn and hold in back, k2, p1 from cn.

2 over 1 Left Purl Cross (2/1 LPC): Sl 2 to cn and hold in front, p1, k2 from cn.

2 over 2 Left Cross (2/2 LC): Sl 2 sts to cn and hold in front, k2, k2 from cn.

Slip, slip, purl (ssp): Slip next 2 sts 1 at a time kwise, slip sts back to LH needle and p2tog-tbl.

Row 14: K4, p3, k1, p2, k4.
Row 15: P4, 2/1 LPC, 2/1 RPC, p4.
Row 16: K5, p4, k5.
Row 17: P5, 2/2 LC, p5.
Row 18: K5, p4, k5.
Row 19: P5, k4, p5.
Row 20: K5, p4, k5.
Rep Rows 1–20 for pat.

Sweater

Body
With smaller needles and MC, cast on 82 sts.

Work 6 rows in 1x1 rib.

Set-up row (WS): Change to larger needles; [p4, k2, p2, k2] twice, pm, k2, p2, k2, p4, k2, p2, k5, p4, k5, p2, k2, p4, k2, p2, k2, pm, [k2, p2, k2, p4] twice.

Row 1 (RS): Work 4 sts in Moss St, p2, work 2-st Mini-Cable, p2, work 4-st Oval Cable, p2, 1/1 RC, p4, work 2-st Mini-Cable, p2, work 4-st Oval Cable, p2, work 2-st Mini-Cable, work 14-st Diamond Moss Panel, work 2-st Mini-Cable, p2, work 4-st Oval Cable, p2, work 2-st Mini-Cable, p4, work 2-st Mini-Cable, p2, work 4-st Oval Cable, p2, 1 work 2-st Mini-Cable, p2, work 4 sts in Moss St.

Work even in established pats, knitting the knit sts and purling the purl sts on WS rows, until piece measures 3½ inches, ending with a WS row.

Left Back
Work to first marker, turn, leaving rem sts unworked.

Work even on these 20 sts until armhole measures 3 inches, ending with a WS row.

Transfer first 8 sts to waste yarn for back neck and last 12 sts to separate waste yarn for shoulder.

Front
With RS facing, rejoin yarn; work to next marker, turn, leaving rem 20 sts unworked.

Work even on these 42 sts until armhole measures 2 inches, ending with a WS row.

Shape Neck
Row 1 (RS): Work 17 sts; transfer next 8 sts to waste yarn for front neck; join 2nd ball of yarn and work last 17 sts.

Row 2 (WS): Working both sides at once, work to 2 sts before neck edge, ssp; p2tog, work to end—16 sts each side.

Pattern Stitches

Moss St (even number of sts)
Rows 1 (RS) and 2: *K1, p1; rep from *.
Rows 3 and 4: *P1, k1; rep from *.
Rep Rows 1–4 for pattern.

Oval Cable (4 sts)
Row 1 (RS): 1/1 RC, 1/1 LC.
Row 2: P4.
Row 3: 1/1 LC, 1/1 RC.
Row 4: P4.
Rep Rows 1–4 for pat.

Mini-Cable (2 sts)
Row 1 (RS): 1/1 RC.
Row 2: P2.
Row 3: K2.
Row 4: P2.
Rep Rows 1–4 for pat.

Diamond Moss Panel (14-st panel)
Note: A chart is provided for those preferring to work pat st from a chart.
Row 1 (RS): P5, 2/2 LC, p5.
Row 2: K5, p4, k5.
Row 3: P4, 2/1 RC, 2/1 LPC, p4.
Row 4: K4, p2, k1, p3, k4.
Row 5: P3, 2/1 RC, p1, k1, 2/1 LPC, p3.
Row 6: K3, p2, k1, p1, k1, p3, k3.
Row 7: P2, 2/1 RC, [p1, k1] twice, 2/1 LPC, p2.
Row 8: K2, p2, [k1, p1] twice, k1, p3, k2.
Row 9: P2, k2, [p1, k1] 3 times, k2, p2.
Row 10: K2, p3, [k1, p1] twice, k1, p2, k2.
Row 11: P2, 2/1 LPC, [p1, k1] twice, 2/1 RPC, p2.
Row 12: K3, p3, k1, p1, k1, p2, k3.
Row 13: P3, 2/1 LPC, p1, k1, 2/1 RPC, p3.

Row 3: Work to 2 sts before neck edge, k2tog; ssk, work to end—15 sts each side.

Rows 4–6: Rep Rows 2 and 3, ending with Row 2—12 sts each side.

Work even until armhole measures 3 inches, ending with a WS row.

Cut yarns and transfer sts to waste yarn.

Right Back
With RS facing, rejoin yarn.

Work even until armhole measures 3 inches, ending with a WS row.

Transfer first 12 sts to waste yarn for shoulder and last 8 sts to separate waste yarn for back neck.

Sleeves
With smaller needles and MC, cast on 42 sts.

Work 6 rows in 1x1 rib.

Set-up row (WS): Change to larger needles; p4, k2, p4, k2, p2, k5, p4, k5, p2, k2, p4, k2, p4.

Row 1 (RS): Work 4 sts in Moss St, p2, work 4-st Oval Cable, p2, work 2-st Mini-Cable, work 14-sts Diamond Moss Panel, work 2-st Mini-Cable, p2, work 4-st Oval Cable, p2, work 4 sts in Moss St.

Work even in established pats, knitting the knit sts and purling the purl sts on WS rows, until piece measures 3½ inches, ending with a WS row.

Bind off loosely.

Finishing
Join shoulders using 3-needle bind-off (see Lesson 3 on page 12).

Right Back Band
With smaller needles and MC, beg at top, pick up and knit 42 sts along right-back edge.

Work 5 rows in 1x1 rib.

Bind off loosely in pat.

Left Back Band
With smaller needles and MC, beg at bottom, pick up and knit 42 sts along left-back edge.

Work 1 row in 1x1 rib.

Buttonhole row (RS): [K1, p1] twice, k1, *yo, k2tog, [p1, k1] 3 times; rep from * 3 times, yo, k2tog, p1, k1, p1.

Work 3 rows in 1x1 rib.

Bind off loosely in pat. Do not cut yarn.

Collar
With RS facing and using same yarn, pick up and knit 5 sts along band, k8 back neck sts, pick up and knit 11 sts along left neck edge, k8 front neck sts, pick up and knit 11 sts along right neck edge, k8 back neck sts—51 sts.

Work 1x1 rib for 2½ inches.

Bind off loosely in pat.

Sew sleeves to armhole openings. Sew sleeve seams.

Sew buttons to right back band opposite buttonholes.

Skirt
With larger needles and CC, cast on 95 sts.

Beg with a RS row, work 5 rows in St st.

Turning ridge (WS): Knit.

Next row: Cast on 4 sts, knit to end—99 sts.

Work even until piece measures 6½ inches from turning ridge, ending with a WS row.

Dec row (RS): [K7, k2tog] 11 times—88 sts.

Work 5 rows even.

Turning ridge (RS): K4, then drop these sts from needle; purl to end—84 sts.

Work 5 rows in St st.

Bind off loosely.

Finishing

Fringe

Unravel the 4 dropped sts all the way down to cast-on edge.

*Make overhand knot with 2 loops; rep from * until all loops are knotted tog in sets of 2.

Cut the ends of the loops to make the fringe.

Fold the bottom hem up at the turning ridge. Sew cast-on edge to WS.

Rep for top waist band and bind-off edge.

Fold skirt so that edges overlap creating an 11½-inch waist (fringe will be at side of front). Sew 2 snap closures to inside of waist band to secure this fit. ●

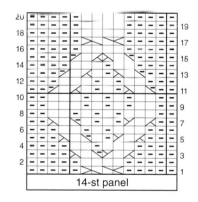

DIAMOND MOSS PANEL

14-st panel

STITCH KEY

☐ K on RS, p on WS

— P on RS, k on WS

2/1 RC

2/1 RPC

2/1 LPC

2/2 LC

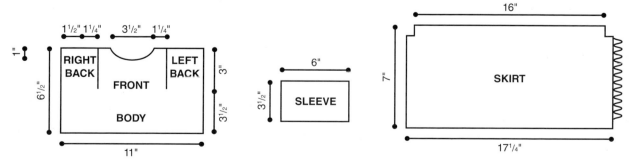

Lesson 6: Color Your World Easy With the Duplicate Stitch

You don't need to learn any fancy stranded colorwork stitches to add some quick color to your project. The duplicate stitch that is used on the Duplicate Debbie outfit, page 31, is created on the knit side of the fabric because it follows the "v" of each stitch, which essentially "duplicates" the stitch below with a new color of yarn. The beauty of this method is that you can add color as an "afterthought" to your project if you feel your design needs a little excitement. Follow these simple steps and you'll be adding color to your world in no time!

The duplicate stitch is an embroidery stitch that mimics the actual knitted stitches of a finished piece to add color and pattern to the surface.

Avoid knots on the wrong side of your work by weaving in the tail.

Step 1: Bring the threaded needle to the front of the work at the bottom V of a knit stitch.

Step 2: Follow the path of that stitch by inserting the needle behind the 2 legs of the stitch above.

Step 3: Insert the needle back through the original point.

Repeat Steps 2 and 3, referring to the illustrations below, in any direction you like, always following the path of the knitted stitches.

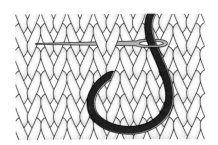

Duplicate Debbie

Finished Measurements
Chest: 12½ inches
Sweater length: 6 inches
Pants length: 10 inches

Materials
- Red Heart Soft Yarn (worsted weight; 100% acrylic; 256 yds/140g per ball): 1 ball each pink #6768 (A), white #4600 (B), lavender #3720 (C) and plummy #9940 (D)
- Size 5 (3.75mm) 16-inch circular and double-point needles (set of 5)
- Size 7 (4.5mm) 16-inch circular and double-point needles (set of 5) or size needed to obtain gauge
- Stitch markers
- Bobbins (optional)
- 4 snap closures
- 12 inches ⅛-inch-wide elastic

Gauge
20 sts and 25 rows/rnds = 4 inches/10cm in St st with larger needles.

To save time, take time to check gauge.

Special Abbreviations
Make 1 Left (M1L): Insert LH needle from front to back under the running thread between the last st worked and next st on LH needle; knit into the back of resulting loop.

Make 1 Right (M1R): Insert LH needle from back to front under the running thread between the last st worked and next st on LH needle. With RH needle, knit into the front of resulting loop.

Pattern Notes
When working raglan yoke, work each set of stitches using different balls/bobbins of A and B, using the intarsia method. Always bring new color up and around old color to twist yarns and prevent holes.

Pants are worked from the waist down.

Sweater

Lower Body

With smaller circular needle and A, cast on 61 sts. Do not join.

Knit 2 rows.

Change to larger needle; beg with a WS (purl) row, work in St st until piece measures 3 inches, ending with a RS row.

Next row (WS): P12 back sts, bind off 6 underarm sts, p25 front sts (including st rem on RH needle after last bind-off), bind off underarm 6 sts, p12 back sts. Do not cut yarn.

Transfer sts to separate pieces of waste yarn.

Sleeves

With smaller circular needle and B, cast on 24 sts. Do not join.

Knit 2 rows.

Change to larger needle; beg with a WS (purl) row, work in St st until piece measures 2½ inches, ending with a WS row.

Bind off 3 sts at beg of next 2 rows—18 sts.

Transfer sts to waste yarn. Do not cut yarn.

Rep for 2nd sleeve.

Raglan Yoke & Front Neck

Set-up row (RS): With larger circular needle and A, k12 back sts, pm; with B, k18 sleeve sts, pm; with A, k25 front sts, pm; with B, k18 sleeve sts, pm; with A, k12 back sts—85 sts.

Row 2 (WS): Purl across, maintaining established color sequence.

Row 3 (dec): *Knit to 2 sts before marker, k2tog, slip marker, ssk; rep from * 3 more times, knit to end—77 sts.

Row 4: Work even.

Rows 5–12: Rep [Rows 3 and 4] 4 times—45 sts.

Row 13: Mark 5 center front sts; maintaining color sequence and continuing raglan decs at each marker, work to 5 marked sts; transfer 5 marked sts to waste yarn for front neck, join new strand of A and complete row—32 sts with 16 sts each side of neck.

Row 14: Purl.

Rows 15–18: Rep raglan decs before and after markers [every RS row] twice and at the same time, dec 1 at each neck edge once ending with a WS row—7 sts each side. Cut yarns.

Finishing
Weave in ends. Block as desired.

Neck Band
Row 1 (RS): With smaller needle and B, k7, pick up and knit 5 sts along neck edge, k5 front neck sts, pick and knit 5 along neck edge, k7—29 sts.

Row 2: Knit.

Bind off loosely, but do not cut yarn.

Left Back Band
Using same yarn, pick up and knit 32 sts along left back edge.

Knit 1 row.

Bind off loosely.

Right Back Band
With smaller needle and B, and beg at bottom, pick up and knit 32 sts along right back edge.

Knit 1 row.

Bind off loosely.

Sew 4 snap closures evenly spaced along back bands.

With tapestry needle and C, follow chart to duplicate st a heart in the center front yoke.

Pants
With smaller dpns and D, cast on 60 sts; mark beg of rnd and join, being careful not to twist sts. Knit 5 rnds.

Turning ridge: Purl around.

Knit 5 rnds.

Change to larger dpns; work in St st until piece measures 2 inches from turning ridge.

Inc rnd: K29, M1L, k1, M1R, k30—62 sts.

Knit 3 rnds.

Inc rnd: K30, M1L, k1, M1R, k31—64 sts.

Knit 3 rnds.

Inc rnd: K31, M1L, k1, M1R, k32—66 sts.

Knit 3 rnds.

Inc rnd: K32, M1L, k1R, M1, k33—68 sts.

Work even until piece measures 5 inches from turning ridge.

Left Leg
Rnd 1: K34, leaving rem sts unworked on a dpn or waste yarn; distribute left leg sts on 3 dpns, mark beg of rnd and join.

Work in St st until leg measures 4¾ inches.

Change to smaller dpns; knit 1 rnd, purl 1 rnd.

Bind off loosely.

Right Leg
Work as for left leg.

Finishing
Overlap ends of elastic and sew tog to make an 11-inch circle. Fold waist hem down along turning ridge covering elastic. Sew hem in place. •

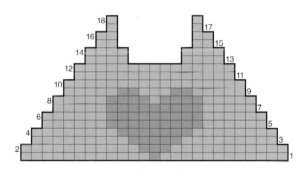

DUPLICATE ST CHART

COLOR KEY	
	A (already knit)
	Duplicate st with C over A

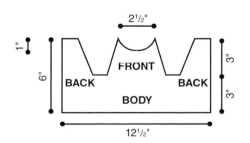

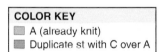

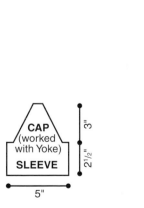

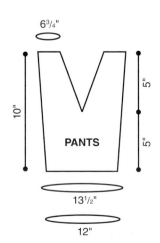

Lesson 7: Delightful Embroidered Accents

Adding simple embroidered details can add excitement and dimension to your knitted creations. Embroidery Emma robe and slippers use the easy outline stitch, lazy daisy stitch and French knot. Once you learn these simple-to-understand stitches, there's no limit to the variety of accents you can create!

Lazy Daisy

Thread the tapestry needle with desired yarn. From the wrong side, bring the needle up through to the right side. Form the yarn into a loop, go back through a stitch next to where the yarn originally came through. Do not pull the loop tight. Keeping the loop shape, bring the needle back up again from the wrong side and to the right side inside the loop. Cross over the top of the loop and go back through to the wrong side just outside the loop.

French Knot

Thread the tapestry needle with desired yarn. From the wrong side, bring the needle up through to the right side. Wrap the yarn around the needle three times. Go back through a stitch next to where the yarn originally came through. Holding the yarn tight with your fingers, pull the needle through the wraps and to the back of the work.

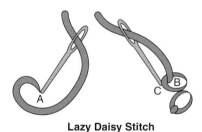

Lazy Daisy Stitch

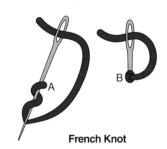

French Knot

Outline Stitch

Thread the tapestry needle with desired yarn. From the wrong side, bring the needle up through the work to the right side. Make a short stitch while holding the loop of yarn off to one side. Bring the needle halfway back along the stitch formed and pull the first stitch into place.

Outline Stitch

Embroidery Emma

Finished Measurements
Chest: 15½ inches
Length: 11 inches

Materials
- Plymouth Yarn Adore (super bulky weight; 100% nylon; 74 yds/ 50g per ball): 3 balls tangerine #13
- Size 10 (6mm) double-point (set of 4) and straight needles or size needed to obtain gauge
- Size J/10 (6mm) crochet hook
- Stitch marker
- Colorful scrap yarn for embroidery

6 SUPER BULKY

Gauge
13 sts and 6 rows = 4 inches/10cm in garter st.

To save time, take time to check gauge.

Pattern Note
Body of robe is worked back and forth in one piece. After shoulders are joined, sleeves are picked up from armhole and worked in the round to the cuff.

Robe

Body
With straight needles, cast on 50 sts.

Work in garter st for 8 inches, ending with a WS row.

Next row (RS): K15; turn, leaving rem 35 sts unworked.

Right Front and Collar
Work even on these 15 sts until armhole measures 3 inches, ending with a WS row.

Next row (RS): K9 for collar; transfer rem 6 sts to waste yarn for shoulder.

Work even until collar measures 1½ inches.

Place collar sts on waste yarn.

Back

With RS facing; rejoin yarn.

Work in garter st on next 20 sts until armhole measures 3 inches, ending with a RS row.

Next row (WS): K6, bind off 8, k6.

Place sts on waste yarn for shoulders.

Left Front & Collar

With RS facing, rejoin yarn.

Work rem 15 sts in garter st until armhole measures 3 inches, ending with a RS row.

Next row (WS): K9 for collar; transfer rem 6 sts to waste yarn for shoulder.

Work even until collar measures 1½ inches.

Place collar sts on waste yarn.

Transfer shoulder sts to dpns, then join shoulders using 3-needle bind-off (see Lesson 3 on page 12).

Sleeve

With RS facing, using dpns and starting at center underarm, pick up and knit 20 sts evenly spaced around armhole; mark beg of rnd and join.

Work in garter st (purl 1 rnd, knit 1 rnd) until sleeve measures 4 inches.

Bind off loosely.

Finishing

Transfer collar sts to dpns.

Join collar sts using 3-needle bind-off.

Sew collar to back of neck.

Weave in ends.

Embellishment
Referring to photo and using scrap yarn, embroider a flower on collar.

Belt
Cast on 5 sts.

Work in garter st for 34 inches.

Bind off loosely.

Slippers

Sole
With dpns, cast on 5 sts.

Work in garter st for 2¾ inches.

Rnd 1: With RS facing and using first dpn, k5; with 2nd dpn, pick up and knit 7 sts along side and 2 sts in cast-on edge; with 3rd dpn, pick up and knit 2 sts in cast-on edge, then 7 sts along side; mark beg of rnd and join—23 sts.

Rnds 2 and 3: Knit.

Shape Toe

Rnd 1: K2tog, k1, k2tog, knit to end—21 sts.

Rnd 2: Knit.

Rnd 3: K3tog, knit to end—19 sts.

Rnd 4: Knit 1 rnd.

Rnd 5 (eyelet rnd): K1, [yo, k2tog] 9 times.

Rnds 6 and 7: Knit.

Bind off loosely.

Tie

With crochet hook, make a chain for 20 inches.

Tie each end in a secure knot.

Weave chain through eyelet holes of slippers. ●

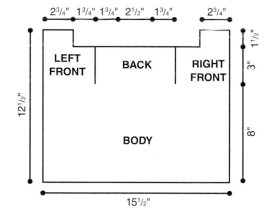

General Information

Abbreviations & Symbols

[ ] work instructions within brackets as many times as directed

( ) work instructions within parentheses in the place directed

** repeat instructions following the asterisks as directed

* repeat instructions following the single asterisk as directed

" inch(es)

approx approximately
beg begin/begins/beginning
CC contrasting color
ch chain stitch
cm centimeter(s)
cn cable needle
dec(s) decrease/decreases/ decreasing
dpn(s) double-point needle(s)
g gram(s)
inc(s) increase/increases/ increasing

k knit
k2tog knit 2 stitches together
kfb knit in front and back
kwise knitwise
LH left hand
m meter(s)
M1 make one stitch
MC main color
mm millimeter(s)
oz ounce(s)
p purl
p2tog purl 2 stitches together
pat(s) pattern(s)
pm place marker
psso pass slipped stitch over
pwise purlwise
rem remain/remains/remaining
rep(s) repeat(s)
rev St st reverse stockinette stitch
RH right hand
rnd(s) rounds
RS right side

skp slip, knit, pass slipped stitch over—1 stitch decreased
sk2p slip 1, knit 2 together, pass slipped stitch over the knit 2 together—2 stitches decreased
sl slip
sl 1 kwise slip 1 knitwise
sl 1 pwise slip 1 purlwise
sl st slip stitch(es)
ssk slip, slip, knit these 2 stitches together—a decrease
st(s) stitch(es)
St st stockinette stitch
tbl through back loop(s)
tog together
WS wrong side
wyib with yarn in back
wyif with yarn in front
yd(s) yard(s)
yfwd yarn forward
yo (yo's) yarn over(s)

Skill Levels

BEGINNER

Beginner projects for first-time knitters using basic stitches. Minimal shaping.

EASY

Easy projects using basic stitches, repetitive stitch patterns, simple color changes and simple shaping and finishing.

INTERMEDIATE

Intermediate projects with a variety of stitches, mid-level shaping and finishing.

EXPERIENCED

Experienced projects using advanced techniques and stitches, detailed shaping and refined finishing.

Standard Yarn Weight System
Categories of yarn, gauge ranges and recommended needle sizes.

Yarn Weight Symbol & Category Names	**0** LACE	**1** SUPER FINE	**2** FINE	**3** LIGHT	**4** MEDIUM	**5** BULKY	**6** SUPER BULKY
Type of Yarns in Category	Fingering 10-Count Crochet Thread	Sock, Fingering, Baby	Sport, Baby	DK, Light Worsted	Worsted, Afghan, Aran	Chunky, Craft, Rug	Super Chunky, Roving
Knit Gauge Range* in Stockinette Stitch to 4 inches	33–40 sts**	27–32 sts	23–26 sts	21–24 sts	16–20 sts	12–15 sts	6–11 sts
Recommended Needle in Metric Size Range	1.5–2.25mm	2.25–3.25mm	3.25–3.75mm	3.75–4.5mm	4.5–5.5mm	5.5–8mm	8mm and larger
Recommended Needle U.S. Size Range	000 to 1	1 to 3	3 to 5	5 to 7	7 to 9	9 to 11	11 and larger

* **GUIDELINES ONLY:** The above reflect the most commonly used gauges and needle sizes for specific yarn categories.

** Lace weight yarns are usually knitted on larger needles and hooks to create lacy, openwork patterns. Accordingly, a gauge range is difficult to determine. Always follow the gauge stated in your pattern.

Inches Into Millimeters & Centimeters
All measurements are rounded off slightly.

inches	mm	cm	inches	cm	inches	cm	inches	cm
⅛	3	0.3	5	12.5	21	53.5	38	96.5
¼	6	0.6	5½	14	22	56.0	39	99.0
⅜	10	1.0	6	15.0	23	58.5	40	101.5
½	13	1.3	7	18.0	24	61.0	41	104.0
⅝	15	1.5	8	20.5	25	63.5	42	106.5
¾	20	2.0	9	23.0	26	66.0	43	109.0
⅞	22	2.2	10	25.5	27	68.5	44	112.0
1	25	2.5	11	28.0	28	71.0	45	114.5
1¼	32	3.2	12	30.5	29	73.5	46	117.0
1½	38	3.8	13	33.0	30	76.0	47	119.5
1¾	45	4.5	14	35.5	31	79.0	48	122.0
2	50	5.0	15	38.0	32	81.5	49	124.5
2½	65	6.5	16	40.5	33	84.0	50	127.0
3	75	7.5	17	43.0	34	86.5		
3½	90	9.0	18	46.0	35	89.0		
4	100	10.0	19	48.5	36	91.5		
4½	115	11.5	20	51.0	37	94.0		

Knitting Basics

Long-Tail Cast-On

Leaving an end about an inch long for each stitch to be cast on, make a slip knot on the right needle.

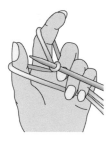

Place the thumb and index finger of your left hand between the yarn ends with the long yarn end over your thumb, and the strand from the skein over your index finger. Close your other fingers over the strands to hold them against your palm. Spread your thumb and index fingers apart and draw the yarn into a "V."

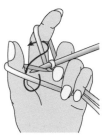

Place the needle in front of the strand around your thumb and bring it underneath this strand. Carry the needle over and under the strand on your index finger.

Draw through loop on thumb.

Drop the loop from your thumb and draw up the strand to form a stitch on the needle.

Repeat until you have cast on the number of stitches indicated in the pattern. Remember to count the beginning slip knot as a stitch.

Knit (K)

Insert tip of right needle from front to back in next stitch on left needle.

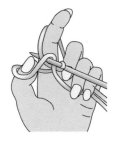

Bring yarn under and over the tip of the right needle.

Pull yarn loop through the stitch with right needle point.

Slide the stitch off the left needle. The new stitch is on the right needle.

Purl (P)

With yarn in front, insert tip of right needle from back to front through next stitch on the left needle.

Bring yarn around the right needle counterclockwise. With right needle, draw yarn back through the stitch.

Slide the stitch off the left needle.

The new stitch is on the right needle.

Bind-Off

Binding Off (Knit)

Knit first two stitches on left needle. Insert tip of left needle into first stitch worked on right needle and pull it over the second stitch and completely off the needle.

Knit the next stitch and repeat. When one stitch remains on right needle, cut yarn and draw tail through last stitch to fasten off.

Binding Off (Purl)

Purl first two stitches on left needle. Insert tip of left needle into first stitch worked on right needle and pull it over the second stitch and completely off the needle.

Purl the next stitch and repeat. When one stitch remains on right needle, cut yarn and draw tail through last stitch to fasten off.

Invisible Increase (M1)

There are several ways to make or increase one stitch.

Make 1 With Left Twist (M1L)

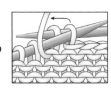

Insert left needle from front to back under the horizontal loop between the last stitch worked and next stitch on left needle.

With right needle, knit into the back of this loop.

To make this increase on the purl side, insert left needle in same manner and purl into the back of the loop.

Make 1 With Right Twist (M1R)

Insert left needle from back to front under the horizontal loop between the last stitch worked and next stitch on left needle.

With right needle, knit into the front of this loop.

To make this increase on the purl side, insert left needle in same manner and purl into the front of the loop.

Make 1 With Backward Loop Over the Right Needle

With your thumb, make a loop over the right needle.

Slip the loop from your thumb onto the needle and pull to tighten.

Make 1 in Top of Stitch Below

Insert tip of right needle into the stitch on left needle one row below.

Knit this stitch, then knit the stitch on the left needle.

Decrease (Dec)

Knit 2 Together (K2tog)

Put tip of right needle through next two stitches on left needle as to knit. Knit these two stitches as one.

Purl 2 Together (P2tog)

Put tip of right needle through next two stitches on left needle as to purl. Purl these two stitches as one.

Slip, Slip, Knit (Ssk)

Slip next two stitches, one at a time as to knit, from left needle to right needle.

Insert left needle in front of both stitches and knit them together.

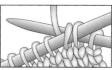

Slip, Slip, Purl (Ssp)

Slip next two stitches, one at a time, as to knit from left needle to right needle. Slip these stitches back onto left needle keeping them twisted. Purl these two stitches together through back loops.

Backward-Loop Cast-On

This is the first cast-on that many knitters learn. It's very easy to do, but the first row is a little challenging to work. It's a handy one to use if you need to cast on stitches at the beginning or end of a row.

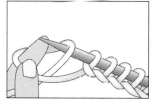

Step 1: Pick up the working yarn with your left hand to create a loop.

Step 2: Twist the loop around a half turn to the right, until it crosses over itself.

Step 3: Put the loop on the needle and pull the working yarn to tighten.

Pick Up & Knit

Step 1: With right side facing, working 1 st in from edge, insert tip of needle in space between first and second stitch.

Step 2: Wrap yarn around needle.

Step 3: Pull loop through to front.

Step 4: Repeat Steps 1–3.

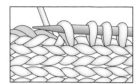

I-Cord

Use 2 double-point needles. Cast on (backward-loop method) number of sts indicated. *Knit across. Do not turn. Slip sts to other end of needle. Repeat from * until I-cord is desired length. Bind off or thread yarn through sts to end.

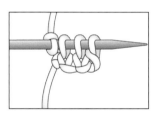

Intarsia

In certain patterns there are larger areas of color within the piece. Since this type of pattern requires a new color only for that section, it is not necessary to carry the yarn back and forth across the back. For this type of color change, a separate ball of yarn or bobbin is used for each section of color, making the yarn available only where needed.

Before beginning the project, wind a bobbin for each color area, allowing ¾ inch for each stitch plus 10 inches extra to weave in at beginning and end of color section.

Bring the new yarn being used up and around the yarn just worked; this will twist, or "lock" the colors and prevent holes from occurring at the join. The top drawing shows how the two colors are twisted on the wrong side of the work and the bottom drawing shows what the pattern looks like from the front.

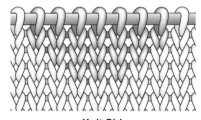

Knit Side

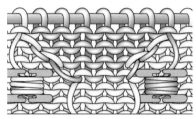

Purl Side

Pompoms

Cut two cardboard circles in size specified in pattern. Cut a hole in the center of each circle, about ½ inch in diameter. Thread a tapestry needle with a length of yarn doubled.

Holding both circles together, insert needle through center hole, over the outside edge, through center again (Figure 1) until entire circle is covered and center hole is filled (thread more length of yarn as needed).

With sharp scissors, cut yarn between the two circles all around the circumference (Figure 2).

Using two 12-inch strands of yarn, slip yarn between circles and overlap yarn ends two or three times (Figure 3) to prevent knot from slipping, pull tightly and tie into a firm knot. Remove cardboard and fluff out pompom by rolling it between your hands. Trim even with scissors, leaving tying ends for attaching pompom to project.

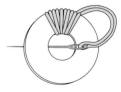

Figure 1

Figure 2

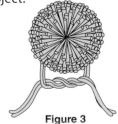

Figure 3

Suppliers

Berroco Inc.
1 Tupperware Drive
Suite 4
North Smithfield, RI 02896-6815
(401) 769-1212
www.berroco.com

Cascade Yarns
1224 Andover Park E.
Tukwila, WA 98188
(206) 574-0440
www.cascadeyarns.com

Coats & Clark
Red Heart Yarns
Consumer Services
P.O. Box 12229
Greenville, SC 29612-0229
(800) 648-1479

Patons
320 Livingstone Ave. S.
Box 40
Listowel, ON
N4W 3H3 Canada

Plymouth Yarn Co.
500 Lafayette St.
Bristol, PA 19007
(215) 788-0459
www.plymouthyarn.com

Universal Yarn Inc.
5991 Caldwell Business Park Drive
Harrisburg, NC 28075
(704) 789-YARN (9276)

Photo Index

5

9

25

13

19

31

37

Easy How-to Techniques For Simply Stylish 18" Dolls is published by Annie's, 306 East Parr Road, Berne, IN 46711. Printed in USA. Copyright © 2012, 2013 Annie's. All rights reserved. This publication may not be reproduced in part or in whole without written permission from the publisher.

RETAIL STORES: If you would like to carry this pattern book or any other Annie's publications, visit AnniesWSL.com.

Every effort has been made to ensure that the instructions in this pattern book are complete and accurate. We cannot, however, take responsibility for human error, typographical mistakes or variations in individual work. Please visit AnniesCustomerCare.com to check for pattern updates.

ISBN: 978-1-59635-730-3
3 4 5 6 7 8 9

1064

YRNBK

EAN   ISBN: 978-1-59635-730-3

5 1 1 9 5

9 781596 357303

Ways to Save the Planet Before Bedtime

You can do
these anytime—
not just before you
go to bed! It doesn't take a
superhero to save the world...

JUST YOU!

Paul Mason

Text and illustrations © Pearson Education Limited, 2016.

This edition of *68 Ways to Save the Planet Before Bedtime* is published by Pearson Education Inc. by arrangement with Pearson Education Limited. All rights reserved. Printed in Mexico.

Acknowledgments

We would like to thank the children and teachers of Bangor Central Integrated Primary School, NI; Bishop Henderson C of E Primary School, Somerset; Brookside Community Primary School, Somerset; Cheddington Combined School, Buckinghamshire; Cofton Primary School, Birmingham; Dair House Independent School, Buckinghamshire; Deal Parochial School, Kent; Newbold Riverside Primary School, Rugby and Windmill Primary School, Oxford for their invaluable help in the development and trialling of the Bug Club resources.

Original illustrations © Pearson Education 2011
Illustrated by Jeff Edwards, The Boy Fitz Hammond and David Oakley

The right of Paul Mason to be identified as author of this work has been asserted by him in accordance with the Copyright, Designs and Patents Act 1988.

Photographs:
Pearson Education Ltd: 2-3, 6-7, 14-15, 14-15l, 14-15c, 14-15cl, 14-15cr, 14-15r, 18-19, 22-23.

All other images © Pearson Education

Printed in Mexico

ISBN-13: 978-0-328-83285-9
ISBN-10:   0-328-83285-5
2 3 4 5 6 7 8 9 10 V0B4 19 18 17 16 15